# Too Numerous

• • • • • • • • • •

# Too Numerous

## KENT SHAW

University of Massachusetts Press

AMHERST AND BOSTON

Copyright © 2019 by University of Massachusetts Press
All rights reserved
Printed in the United States of America

ISBN 978-1-62534-430-4 (paper)

Designed by Sally Nichols
Set in Adobe Garamond Pro and Alternate Gothic
Printed and bound by Maple Press, Inc.

Cover design by Patricia Duque Campos
Cover art by Julie Mehretu, *Stadia 1*, 2004 (detail)
Ink and acrylic on canvas, 107 in. x 140 in. / (271.78 cm x 355.6 cm)
© Julie Mehretu

Library of Congress Cataloging-in-Publication Data

Names: Shaw, Kent, 1971– author.
Title: Too numerous / Kent Shaw.
Description: Amherst : University of Massachusetts Press, [2019] |
Identifiers: LCCN 2018051835 (print) | LCCN 2018056365 (ebook) |
ISBN 9781613766804 (ebook) | ISBN 9781613766811 (ebook) |
ISBN 9781625344304 | ISBN 9781625344304 (paperback)
Subjects:  LCSH: American prose literature—21st century.
Classification: LCC PS3619.H3937 (ebook) | LCC PS3619.H3937 A6 2019 (print) |
DDC 814/.6—dc23
LC record available at https://lccn.loc.gov/2018051835

British Library Cataloguing-in-Publication Data
A catalog record for this book is available from the British Library.

# Contents

# Acknowledgments

*Bennington Review:* "There were bricks put at brick angles"

*Cincinnati Review:* "My fear is that someone would invent a tool to untether me"

*Denver Quarterly:* "Actually, this poem belongs to my wife"

*Guernica:* "Now I understand what maturity is. Thank you, wool!"

*Handsome Magazine:* "How high technology might one day be indispensable to our lives"

*Hayden's Ferry Review:* "The boxes were arranged so they formed a Leviathan"

*Hobart:* "A story from my romantic past. It was full of misgivings," "The definition of OK when you're only kind of OK"

*Laurel Review:* "The definition of curtail"

*Literary Review:* "To mountainize is a verb"

*Memorious:* "My city is not called Ladders," "Really, there is no end to ambition"

*Michigan Quarterly Review:* "The history I'm living in right now!"

*New Orleans Review:* "They would excavate stones and then rearrange the stones in a city like they appeared in the earth"

*Oversound:* "How to rule out probability"

*Phantom Limb:* "What we do when we wamt to elect a Frank Lloyd Wright," "An ellipsis could be what language is like when it's styrofoam"

*Salt Hill:* "I was born a bass drum. Not a catapult," "This is how ambition looks when it's blooming"

*Southeast Review:* "I'm sorry if the rain was always making your life more confusing"

*Spark & Echo:* "Why God keeps making conviction so easy"

*Third Coast:* "In praise of discipline"

*TYPO:* "People don't understand what an emotion normally looks like"

*upstreet:* "When your middle age is in the middle beginning"

*Vinyl Poetry:* "What we did about a world that kept getting very loud"

*Western Humanities Review:* "Any man can make love for 40 days, if he's making love to himself," "Maybe this city needs more men who are not imitations of the man they hate me for not being"

# Too Numerous

· · · · · · · · ·

# The complicated version of unanimity is actually the quiet kind

. . . . . . . . . . . . . . . . . . . . . . . . . . . . . . . . . .

Our purpose was building boxes and stacking boxes, and then we were holding the boxes
    against the mountain
so that some could live inside their own box.
They were swans shaped out of boxes.
They were insects, many different kinds, living in the corners of boxes.
The rest of us swam in the ocean.
We took the water into our mouths and our eyes and held the water just below our skin
so that we could make our skin look like boxes had been stacked beside our arms and our
    chests.
So goes unanimity. So goes a call to arms among the community.

And the people whose job it was to stand at the top of the mountain looking down were
    not there.
Where were they?
Everything was happening, and at the same time.
We were forming a civilization.
Using a single mountain.
With people pressing their arms into the mountain so the mountain might be mistaken for
    people piled on top of each other.
Boxes, too. With everyone keeping count. Of the types of boxes.
Of shapes they could say boxes looked like. It made the mountain more interesting.

I was swimming through all this. Through the people.
I was feeling like the oceans are feelings, or more than feelings, or more the inside of feelings.
Like if my body was a brown paper bag, and it was inside the ocean, and holding the ocean
    inside it,
you might say the feeling a brown paper bag is having right now is oceaning.
I was oceaning myself. I was doing no harm to myself.

If only I was named David. An ocean named David would seem like something that had a unique personality.

I have built shelves into every level of ocean.

The ocean kept taking them away.

"I am building shelves," I said to the ocean. The ocean kept taking them away.

●

Every civilization is required to be built out of the first stone that existed.

The next stones model the first stone in gesture and contour and mountainside and first leader.

Where did the first leader come from? A stone.

The tenor of his voice sounding a little bit like stone.

The people standing in a crowd will reveal a stone.

And so they build houses. And so they stack boxes.

A man building a stone arch thinks a lot about stone.

Should civilization just be a manner of speaking? Stone thoughts and stone words. Stone etchings.

If nature is certainty, if please is yes,

if equal is a sign to make sure one equals one equals one equals one,

then you understand a row of stones.

And why people use stones to find other stones.

So goes the road to unanimity.

•

Because the invention of boxes begets other boxes, different sized boxes, which are easily
    replicated,
then sent into the middle of a city
where boxes are often waiting with great expectation for the new boxes to arrive.

This is my city. This was my city.
I would never want to get stuck in this city.
I am inescapable in this city. All my friends are sick of me.

Put me in a box. Save me from other boxes.
I am not a mountain. I want to believe I'm a mountain.
I want the city to feel like a set of compartments that keeps growing up around me
so I'll eventually be lost among all the other boxes so numerous the city can safely claim to
    live with numerous purposes.
One of them being me. Another one being boxes sheltering one another from the boxes
that don't know better than to be only numerous.
A city is being invented. A newer city still.
The world that happens where you're looking at the world from the inside.
Like everyone else. We are busy. You're busy.
Unanimity should feel like an ocean subsiding, then gathering itself so that next thing you
    know it's wherever you see.

•

I've been told the hardest stone
is in the earth the hardest stone
appears with the greatest frequency as the hardest stone
in existence the hardest stone
in my daughter's hands looks like the hardest stone
could be mistaken for a weapon against the hardest stone
I might have in our apartment a copy of the hardest stone
it's dark blonde, the hardest stone
with little indentations to make the hardest stone
easier to handle. The hardest stone
as an analogy always fails the hardest stone
is simply the hardest stone
submerged in water, then laid out on the patio furniture to dry the hardest stone
looks and feels like the hardest stone
in my neighbor's hands the hardest stone
is a throat no wonder he admires the hardest stone
I keep in my possession the hardest stone
deemed priceless, or worthless. Personally valuable quantities of the hardest stone
appear at the ocean. The ocean is the hardest stone
in spirit the hardest stone
falls from the sky onto the hardest stone
like thunder. Imagine thunder within the hardest stone.
The hardest stone.
Louder than bombs. Unequal to the hardest stone
in recorded history the hardest stone
was always referred to by name: the hardest stone
could be written upon but not etched with cuneiform or longhand the hardest stone
resisted even the stylus made from the hardest stone
preserved in the earth with the hardest stone
cradling it. A man inherited the hardest stone.
Now he had arms and chest of the hardest stone.
No. I am the hardest stone, a man said.

$\cdots$

# The boxes were arranged so they formed a Leviathan

· · · · · · · · · · · · · · · · · · · · · · · · · · · · · · · ·

As in the dietary tract, the part that you'd crawl through to feel safe, and metamorphosed.

Is it fair to leviathans all over the world if we put this one on display?

Freud made skeptical a whole civilization, so when he died they encased him in a cardboard box.

They labeled it Leviathan.

What would it mean if we built a human out of Freud's mouth?

And the mouthiness was a child?

And the child was a human?

And we put a glass cabinet in the bedroom, and said, Freud's Mouth, this is your childhood?

We would say Freud's Mouth is lucky.

He'll never grow up.

The boxes were arranged so they formed a Leviathan and we said, Good-bye, human child, when he crawled inside them.

There will come a time when civilization has to listen.

Because everything else is so quiet. The forest.

The people who are anxious to be in a fairy tale. Some of them keep their insides well hidden.

I drive by them during my Monday commute.

I am driving through mountains.

These mountains are being held down by a forest, a forest arranged to form a leviathan.

They're mountains that are being metamorphosed.

How lucky is that?

# I'm sorry if the rain was always making your life more confusing

· · · · · · · · · · · · · · · · · · · · · · · · · · · · · · · · · · ·

One problem with forests is they don't care where you are.
They can grow and grow and move around the country. Maybe they'll find you.

I found the forest here. We found each other here.
Beneath the rain. What a talker, that forest.

We kept our engines running like refined petroleum for about three months.
What would "anxious" mean if you couldn't include the definitions of "engine" and "forest"?

My engine is a sensitive construction. A system of Allen wrenches. Tied up to make
    squares.
Allen wrenches aren't supposed to make squares.

The rain is a forest. Left-handed forest, actually.
The clumsy one that exists on certain acreages, where it limped in and then fell asleep.

Rain falling asleep is not as peaceful as you might think.
There is a forest growing where it just rained.

# Any man can make love for 40 days, if he's making love to himself

• • • • • • • • • • • • • • • • • • • • • • • • • • • • • • • • • • •

There was a guy in our neighborhood who attached a series of love letters to a burning tire.
The letters were clumsy.
The kind that a young man would send to his pen pal
when she started making it clear they were only going to be friends.

We were standing with him on the porch,
because he wanted to tell us what he was all about.
He was aspiring. And energetic.
And even though it was kind of early, and my wife would have rather been inside with
    the cats,
we watched. He'd glue-gunned the letters individually to coat hangers and then stuck them
    into the tire.
Of course, they caught fire. It was fabulous.
It felt like we were watching a YouTube video of a young man getting angry.
What a spectacle,
especially when you can tell something is going wrong just off-camera.

If only love could be logical.
Because when you're in love, you're doing something all the time. Like your body's an
    engine.
In one week the guy was signing up to run a half-marathon.
He was going to publish a newspaper.
And then, in November, he was on the ballot for county commissioner as a Green Party
    candidate.
He was dedicated. Like a tire burning while it rolls down a cobblestone street.

40 days symbolizes a long time in the Bible.
So he'd written love letters for the last 40 days.
And he recited a single psalm while he knelt at his bedside.

He was lost inside his choices.

What do you call a wilderness?

What is waiting? Does a mountain ridge wait? Does the interstate wait for the sun to rise?

Does love ever wait, really?

There are men in this country who have made love for 40 days.

They were making love to themselves.

And, in truth, that's exactly what a love letter is.

A tire that's been set fire to on the dining room table.

Young man, let me explain. No one else is supposed to be watching.

# I imagine most molecular arrangements are indifferent to the system they are participating in

· · · · · · · · · · · · · · · · · · · ·

There are molecules alive in my basement!
They are happening slowly. Like how mold is slow.
The rate of small animals burrowing into concrete is slow.
Maybe a water molecule is slow if it's unaware of the other waters around it.

If I were a molecule, I would be falling in love with everything around me.
How do you plan for the future like this?
How are you supposed to make all those different parts of your life into a whole?
I don't even know the expected lifetime of a molecule.
How can I be populated by molecules and not know this?

If there were any justice in this world the molecules of matter would get to meet with the
    molecules of time.
And they would commiserate on the seeming insignificance of their existence.
How the people of this world just pass them over.
They're nothing.
Only an animal that is stalking its prey is careful enough to think of molecules existing.
A heron standing at the river's edge.
A snake. Pretty much all the time a snake.
And a mountain. I won't forget the singular look of each mountain while the sun rises
    behind it.

# In praise of discipline

. . . . . . . . . . . . . .

A story involving discipline will always be more interesting if it involves a sinewy motion.
Like men who have been posed in a long uniform fire, especially when the fire was set using
   dried kindling.
An army that flares, and bursts, then rages.
For instance, the army arriving at Troy.
I would have been in love to feel every catastrophe at work in that fire.
Men holding men. Men being there for men.
Don't let go, men.
Men on fire should act like they are totally unaware of what they are actually doing.

The soldiers were posed to look like a long line of fire.
This is how you should speak about an army of arms welded to one another and walking
   toward you.
Arms carrying arms.
Arm in arm, like they were friends and fellow soldiers together.

In the navy, we said the army was a huddle of trees. Useless trees, until they're set fire.
All on fire. That's how they're together.
Not a single fire left behind to smolder alone at the roadside.
No brooding, soldiers.
No one cares if you're choking. On your feet. The whole world is on fire.
Don't you know there are things that have to die so other things can stay alive.

•

I went camping two weeks ago. And all night my wife and I had to endure the smoke
from a log that was smoldering somewhere by the beach. Someone had abandoned their
fire. There was a very light wind off the ocean. Which was enough to keep it burning. We
cursed that log all night. It was so alone. What a stupid log. Just die already, log. Die. No
one wants to take responsibility for your stupid mistakes.

# A monument designed for upward mobility

. . . . . . . . . . . . . . . . . . . . . . . . .

It would start with runs of steps. Steps going up. But also going down some.
With a few different levels.
People always say they like the feel of this place. Maybe it's the air.
The walls holding up the insides of the warehouse.
And the trees, too, growing somewhere. There should be pictures of trees breathing in air.
And mannerisms of trees emphasized by the guards.
Who clearly have overpopulated the monument.

"Too many guards!" we started off saying.
But it was a compliment.
I told my sister there might not be room. She would have to wait her turn.
Which was me being the jerk I've always been in our family.

But there really are too many guards. Both in the past tense and the present.
Both in the guarded sense and the belligerent.
It makes the guards very happy.
They are wearing concrete like it's a jungle.
And spats over their boots. And eyeglasses.
Everything to make them feel distant and imposing.

This is a monument designed for mown lawns. And the Industrial Age when looked at
   through history.
There are 80 lbs. of ground beef arranged in rough bouquets at the corners.
And volleyballs, too. Colorful volleyballs.
That's mainly just to make people excited about being there.

•

What did you say to that guard when I asked you for a joke?
What do you do when two or three people look at you and you realize you've been on
    camera for the last 20 minutes?
I told you to quit looking back at the brochure.
You thought you were alone. There was no one around.
And now everyone seems to know who you are.
"We're happy you're here!"
But we don't know whether to look at the screen or at you.
We don't know which of the you's we actually prefer.

*

All the different angles are coming in for a meeting.
They're here to talk about life.
Sections of the monument were prepared solely for angles.
Wide angles. And short ones.
They are here for the sake of experiencing an angle.
Lunch boxes that were packed with all shipments of ground beef.
You'd be surprised at the geometry ground beef can make a person when eaten correctly.

Delivery boxes, too. Or cakes. There are so many different scenarios.
With guards around each one. Waiting to tell us something is wrong.
Here is the color yellow colored in on long ribbons that started out beige.
Here is the audio recording of traumatic events in your life.

I would have opened myself up if it hadn't been there were people behind me.
They were eager to get in. Or at least to get past the beginning part that is mainly long lines.
People being held in one place while they wait for the angle they will be given for holding
    their faces.

# How high technology might one day be indispensable to our lives

· · · · · · · · · · · · · · · ·

The water was having problems with its self-image.
And the really unfortunate thing is that it had no one it could relate to.
A beach. No. A plastic bottle. No.
Psychology. Too abstract.

What do you make of a body of water that's no longer sure it wants to be water?
Does it know we're at a moment of impending crisis,
when the plastic water bottles of this world are getting visibly distressed
about what to expect from their future
if there isn't a self-satisfied, self-confident, self-fulfilling water to fill them?
You can't sell a bottle of water that's half-full.
It doesn't matter what optimism means in your city.

And if water were to give up a whole body of water, where would it end?
Are you aware that the human body is 60% water?
And the brain looks like a sponge because it likes to absorb all the water you ingest while
    you're drinking?
And that, in winter, your hands will get cold because there is water inside them actually
    freezing your joints into place?

Please, water, don't give up. How is the human body to fill out its corners?
I am notified every day that refills on inkjet cartridges are at their lowest price ever.
The emails are so inventive. Who would have thought to see inkjet like that!

Does it matter that all I can afford are the cartridges with black ink?
And that I've opted to settle in for the rest of my life at a 600 dpi grayscale setting?

# Definitions of lucky are too numerous

· · · · · · · · · · · · · · · · · · · · · · ·

An object was drawn first on a piece of paper,
then another piece of paper.
Then arches were drawn. Then the object drew another object on top of it.
It was an envelope. The object wasn't happy with just an envelope.
The object drew fantasy and oblong. The object got sweaty.
The object was my friend.
I was drawing the object on other pieces of paper,
while the object—how does an object get so lucky?—
was modeling in Los Angeles.
It was attracting other objects.
The object was getting very specific.
It was being drawn with fingers and leg rolls and ways of sniffing the air.
The object was getting objectified. Totally objectified.
The Los Angeles airports and freeways and objects were not not.
They were objects.
They said, "I am drawing an object."
It will appear on paper as soon as it arrives.
An object passes other objects in the street. Definitions of lucky are too numerous.

# A story from my romantic past. It was full of misgivings.

Meaning it would always start in a small room that was filled with new carpeting.
And black boxes painted brown.
Like a showroom for people who don't like things.

There were women there, too. Innumerable women.
And they were wearing a type of small animal that coiled around their fingers
and elbows and panty lines. The animals made small figures over their décolletage.
I tied the animals to the radiator pipes. I fed them pretzels cut into small pieces.
I was trying to make them less bashful.

How is it a normal person can sound out whatever they think is being put in parentheses?
I was an OK intellectual. I liked dancing to techno. I had taken a vacation once to
    Nice, France.
I would say I was at least tolerable.
Which was a key to my success in romantic undertakings.

That, and living by myself.
I made dinner by myself. I learned to drink wine by myself after work on Fridays.
I spent longish nights with my hand held above a ventilation duct until a small animal
    would crawl out.
I was hoping for it to be mangled,
or at least lame from climbing through ductwork and half-operational vent fans.
The things we all do for a little attention.

"I have a collection of small animals!" I announced one night at a friend's party.
This might not have been the best headline for my match.com profile.
But I had pillows that were small animals. And recyclable bags that looked vaguely like
    animals.
There were open-wound animals I kept living by putting breath mints into their sores.

Which certainly gave a fresh scent to my apartment.

The scent was called Small Animal with Pedigree.

The real story of my romantic past begins when I learned to go out dressed as a small animal.

I had sewn tiny teeth into my wrist.

I carried a pair of pliers. I carried blueprints of small rooms and the various ductwork feeding into them.

# The definition of curtail

· · · · · · · · · · · · · · ·

The mirrors were inside the theater. Pointing at mirrors. They put in a sky.
And they painted the sky using a Marc Chagall that was the same color as Marc Chagall,
but more sky-like. It was Light! Which is a part of the theater community.
As are prepositions. And applause.
And the people attached to applause.
Imagine if Marc Chagall had painted a sky inside a theater.
And the theater was beautiful.

Would it be possible for me to have the name of the theater painted inside me?
Like I was a European. Or I had European inside of me.
Or I was spelling out all my possible shades of voice and demeanor.
I was projecting myself.
As in, the impression of myself that involves carving out whole parts of myself.

"That's where the sky is" is all that I'm saying. It's inside the theater
that is inside me opening out to the other people, glamorous people, expensive people,
    anonymous people, too.
Mainly anonymous people. Maybe Marc Chagall.

Like if a mirror were pointed at other mirrors and what we were really trying to do
is see what our emotions looked like from every possible angle,
and at first it might seem like it's tragic or disastrous, because our emotions are such serious
    business,
but the emotions we think are possible must be more possible
when there are so many ways of looking at them. I am a theater. I am mirrors
on so many parts of my insides. And the audience loves me.
They love me so much, because they can see themselves while they're doing it.

·

I am a jealous man. I was grown a jealous man.
As in the seeds were planted early.

If psychology were a soil that grew continually darker and richer and evenly polluted as
    time goes on,
if psychologies grew into one anther like the knotted capital letters that begin an
    illuminated manuscript,
or the brasswork at the top of a capitol dome, or the murals on the under part,
where airs are circulating into each other,
and the airs are psychology for each other, holding each other when they need to be held,
for inside any psychology another psychology should be fit,
so psychology could be used to psychology the psychologies making psychology so difficult,
then everyone would feel at last that a deeper side is really even deeper than they had first
    imagined.
The topsoil is so rich in this country,
but that's only the beginning of a very long agricultural history.

•

There is a system of strings I have attached to my insides.
On nights when there is a performance, I organize them into a canopy coming out of my
    chest.
With all the other strings attached to those strings.
How would you feel if you heard a map was leading an audience into your insides
with diagrams describing consequences, and string sequences,
and tangents in all directions at the ends of strings that couldn't possibly be the same strings
    anymore
if they have that many places they're going to.
Aren't all strings engineered to come to an end?

I am someone who needs to feel like he's been connected to whatever is "backstage."
Maybe there's an elaborate grid back there that the strings are tied on to.
And that's how I'll find my way home, where it's just me and my wife.
We've been dealing with strings tangled beneath the sink.
And strings hanging above our mattress connecting me to the home that we're living in.
Can I bring the audience to this performance space? Have they been here all along?
Try waking up in here. All you can see is the middle of the night.
Try keeping track of everything living in this house.

It may be the strings aren't me connecting me to me as much as they are me pulling me
    closer
like a jealous lover. Jealousy is so smothering.
I am inside me. I am a ball of string. I am bundled with string.
I am one of those map-diagrams that keeps expanding so fast it might even surpass the
    three-dimensional capacity
        of the warehouse they're housing diagrams in,
so they're building a warehouse to house that one.
I assure you, there will be a Singularity, I will be there, with strings strung to even stronger
    strings and more capable strings,
and they'll be waving themselves at my face.

•

Most days you can find me at home filling out forms online.

They are so kind to me at the end. Thanking me with exclamation points!

How many new strings can I tie around my wrists?

And if the strings are phrased in the form of a question,

should it give me the feeling my life is rich with possibility?

I could be tied in a chair and held under house arrest.

I could be suspended above my life waiting for it to pass me by.

There is an audience inside me waiting to come out. I have locked them inside.

Please, audience, what's going to happen next?

Is it a comedy? A dark comedy? A tether that just keeps holding me right here the whole
    time?

# There were bricks put at brick angles

. . . . . . . . . . . . . . . . . . . . . . . .

Or, in other words, a population of bricks, new bricks, piled onto bricks, and stones
and creek beds and excavators and the color of excavators when they're digging.
Imagine bricks thrown onto the bare feet of children. Or thrown at their mouths.
Imagine this were all the countries in the world.
Paved over. Laid to bed.

I live in front of a brick house between brick streets
beneath an overpass that cannot sound like anything but brick when the traffic passes by.
There are no children here. We have put them to rest.
The ability to breathe is hardship. It depends on where you are standing.

Are you a choir or a forest?
Or bricks that were fired and baked and built to look like a Midwestern city that mattered
    at some point during the 20th Century.

Why do I live here? Why do I open my valise and take out bricks
before I even talk to the other bricks that have taken up residence here?
I am a living paid out in bricks.
I am a building painted over with bricks the color of bricks and the color of an open mouth
and the dark hole where bricks are waiting with other bricks pregnant inside them.
I am no politician.
Only a burden. A brick bed. A brick box. In my house are many mansions.
And they're crowded by hallways paved over with brick. I'm not sure which way to go.

# The invention of psychology, a swan song

· · · · · · · · · · · · · · · · · · · · · · · · · ·

When psychologists built a zoo to commemorate everything that happens in a
    Midwestern city,
the people promised they could be different.
They built second homes. They added more walls to the homes where they were living.
There were private dinners and backyard barbecues.
But nothing mattered.

The zoo was a line of vending machines that produced a wax animal by pouring hot wax
    on a real animal that was being kept inside the machine.
As in "chimpanzee" wasn't quite the chimpanzee they had in mind
so they poured hot wax on it,
and it screamed like an animal screams to remind you the animal parts are real.
Electricity is real. Machinery is real.
Breakfast at the start of every day is real, too.
But the animals had only animal parts.
What do zoos do with an animal's parts when they're dying?

I have lived with an animal since I was 25 years old.
It started in a studio apartment, wall-to-wall carpeting, and a murphy bed.
A window unit that blocked out the sun.
There was a collection of knotted thread I let accumulate in the corner.
On weekends, I took collect phone calls from the local prison.
There is no animal here, I told them.
But, still, I sent letters to their girlfriends, and sometimes gifts.
Why not? said my psychologist when I told her this story.

My life in the 20th Century was a machine based on inhibitions.
It was a wax lake, and the only place to get comfortable was the bottom of the lake.
The secret: Don't move. Don't even try.

I pretended I was in Kansas the year my mother invited me to meet her there.
Is it possible psychology takes up more than just words?
I would like to explain what was happening then. What was probably going to.
What never didn't.

# Why God keeps making conviction so easy

. . . . . . . . . . . . . . . . . . . . . . . . . .

At first, God made conviction the size of a rabbit's throat.

Which was a matter of poor planning. In the suburbs, a rabbit is meandering and conspicuous.

A rabbit is running through the suburban neighborhoods and we're starting to think that
     they're pests.

Maybe there was a time when they were precocious and vulnerable.

That's when we were children.

Conviction, Lord. The kind like boys after school chasing a rabbit and pinning it to the
     driveway.

Does a rabbit hear the inside of a rabbit?

Does it have a productive dialogue with absolutely terrified or petrified or inconvenienced or
provoked or angry but not angry enough because,

look, it's just boys. But the rabbit can't move. The rabbit is helpless.

And the boys have found something heavy to hold over the rabbit's head.

It's bigger than the rabbit's head!

Are you all seeing all this? Maybe the Lord started explaining conviction but we weren't
     paying attention.

Maybe conviction changed to the size of the heaviest thing in the picture.

Maybe it's the boy who can't let go of what he used to think of rabbits,

but that was before this rabbit.

The other boys are laughing at this rabbit.

Which is definitely easier.

Lord, conviction runs deep. Conviction is plentiful. The shape of young animals running at
     evening.

The shape of evening.

The shape of God being boys, whatever a boy is or the inside of a boy or the inside of many
     boys when they're laughing,

so that one boy feels like it's OK now.

It's a fucking rabbit, already. Don't make it so hard.

# How we found more useful sayings about fences

There are many paths to take you into a city. A city of Brotherly Love. A city to point out
which way is West.
Ours was a city of fence makers. And fence menders.
We assembled fences around trees, to admire their treeness.
A distinguished conifer left on the hillside.
A magnolia alone in the rain.
No one cared. Because the only thing the trees ever did was stand there.

So we built fences around our horses. The ones that we owned.
Then our houses.
We started government initiatives that would feature a fence in every part of our lives.
White picket fences. Chain link fences.
We built a fence around the bluebird in our driveway. Or, more appropriately, a system of
fences surrounding the bird to keep all its bird activities in one place.
We know of your struggles, bird. Please. Keep them to yourself.
Maybe we were learning the mechanics of eagerness.
People invented delicate fences. They used them on infants. And their wives.
And the voices inside old GPSes, because we always figured those voices never actually
intended to be such jerks.
There was a grassroots movement to build fences around the American spirit.
But those weren't fences. Only statistical renderings.

This might be how we started writing a history that was historically aimed at the writing
of history
people didn't want associated with their history, but anyone who studies history will
tell you,
history is neither hindsight nor foresight. It's just higher fences, more elaborate fences,
the kinds of fences that will probably need to be repaired after ten years.

•

In my neighborhood, there are people who spend all Saturday alone on their front porch.
It's awkward walking by them.
Like a capacitor in an electrical circuit collecting the charge from a battery, but I don't know
what the source of the electricity is.
And so we build fences. Populations of fences.
Fenced-in driveways. A fenced-in metal detector for some entertainment.
A Border Fence alive in the sky, because something needs to take over whatever the ozone
was doing.
And if that doesn't work. I'll just shelter myself from the sun beneath migrations of fenced
birds.
And their mutual bird struggles trying to keep those fences afloat.

•

It should be no surprise we discovered languages are fences that barely fence anything in.
Or we keep thinking that if we make language about language long enough we'll eventually
    perfect the art of building fences.
Ladies and gentlemen, I give you the 20th Century.
I give you the ocean teeming with armatures, political speeches, possessive nouns, sensuality,
    my wife sleeping in, day, day, day, day.


An aircraft carrier is a system of fences specifically designed to push the ocean out of a
    sailor's life.
But what idiot would go out to sea never thinking about the ocean?
Every day an ocean. Every day only ocean.
I held ocean in my mouth for the six years of my enlistment. I still wasn't ocean.
There were too many fences. There were too many fences requiring me to build other fences.
But what would this world be if every man no longer had fences that were left to be built?

# Now I understand what maturity is. Thank you, wool!

· · · · · · · · · · · · · · · · · · · · · · · · · · · · · · · · · · · · · · ·

We had been asked to piece together the conspiracy using only wool.
Wool blankets. Wool scarves. Wool pajamas. Government-issued wool.
Laid out end to end. And fitted to each other. Sometimes sewn together.
Some places overlapping. Or piling up.
What do you listen for in a conspiracy?
What do you hear when you're wrapped in wool, laid to rest in wool bedding?

It was suffocating. A wool blanket is suffocating if you're using it correctly.
Try more than one.
Try sleeping with a wool blanket that was cut out to look like arms and legs.
Try living beneath her. Or it. Or them.
All the wool blankets tied up so they hang from the sky.
A wool blanket sky. A night can be suffocating. Too many arms in bed with you.
When is the day? What makes day start?
There are nights in Florida and Texas that are heavier than the day.
A wool blanket is still heavier.
And it's hard when you're breathing in there.

For everyone involved. A wool blanket does not have emotions. It does not register
  compassion.
I hated 1991.
I was living in Florida. There's nothing in Florida.
Many species of heron are native to Florida, but herons don't move.
There is lightning. What does a wool blanket do with lightning? It makes cynicism.
Sometimes it rains.
We were basically being led straight into the 21st Century.
It's hard to have friends in the 21st Century.
Everything I own is made from wool. And connected together. Maybe I love wool.

A wool staircase is so practical. It supposedly breathes. Wool suits at Sears department stores. Wool livery, if I owned horses.

Wool lining the cups I use for my coffee.

What makes day start? What a question. The wool is repeating itself. Perhaps that's how answering works.

# People don't understand what an emotion normally looks like

The human emotions are made of more than just flesh.

They're language. They're the shavings from old growth trees, especially the kind that are beside a river.

They're abstract wire sculptures displayed in the corner.

And no one understands what they stand for.

But, then, people don't understand what an emotion normally looks like.

For instance, the human body is 60% water. Which should make it very mysterious.

Until you get older.

By this time in my life the mysteries have settled so that they're little patties mixed from wood shavings and tender skin and a good deal of water.

I think this is my whole life together,

one emotion I apply to each of my body parts, and each body part proud of how emotional it is.

I should use a metal wire to string them together.

Like I run a metal wire through my left shoulder

and then down to that tender part of the skin that's just above my genitals.

This is for when I'm feeling a little sexy. And it's time to turn off the lights.

What a way to speculate about the laws of nature!

As in, emotions add up until a person starts feeling very emotional.

1 + 2 + 3 + all the things that abound in the sun. That is spring.

1 + 1 + 6 + the TV. That is summer.

Maybe people don't want to know what an emotion normally looks like.

And they're wary of metal wires if they're attaching things.

I should have made the wire a part of my outfit.

But since my Grandmother never thought a boy would need to know how to sew, I'm going to have to just tuck the whole apparatus underneath my jacket.

•

I have used wire to weight my emotions down so the wind will never confuse them for
   chaff.
They are OK to settle among the wheat, or on the cool concrete of the patio, or in a pile of
   dead leaves.
All the days of my life.
What if I hold my hands out and, voila, the patterns in dark silk?
Or I paint my windows with rubber cement?
Or I hold plates just above the table until it is obviously uncomfortable to be doing it?
This is the weight in my soul. Actively speaking. To anyone close by.

Has anyone ever spoken to a tree while it is reaching over the water?
I'd imagine it's uncomfortable. I'd imagine it has some complex emotions.
Is it the Law of God coursing through all the world using the same equation?
Do we say "all the days of its life" because we don't know how to add everything up to
   whatever $x$ it is that equals "this tree is feeling emotional"?

I took a metal wire and pushed it through a young bough that had just budded from when
   it was the beginning of spring.
And the tree grew around it.
That might have been the happiest day of its life.

Because now the tree would be connected to me and my very complex emotions.
We could wait for the eternity and then after that the Apocalypse. We're together, I said. All
   the days of our lives.
Which sounds like a softer way of enduring the Lord.
Oh, Lord, why must You insist we suffer in complexity the sum of Your outrageous
   emotions?

# My city is not called Ladders

· · · · · · · · · · · · · · · · · ·

There is a park built in this city for people who want to show up with their ladders.
A park for people who are always thinking, "Maybe that's my ladder."
My neighbors are buying ladders wherever they shop.
They try putting their ladders sideways so they can walk into their neighbor's bedroom.
   "Hello, neighbor!"
Their ladders have mirrors hung from each rung.
They claim to be in a relationship with the ladder, but it's unclear what that will lead to.

My city prefers to be called Hope. But who is it that's actually hopeful?
People think ladders are hopeful. That's optimistic.

People are living and living and living and living. They are a living thing.
They are a simple organism that prefers looking up.
And over. And around. And into everyone's business.
But not down. We all know it's scary down there!

My city, all you think about are stars.
You are mountains at night blocking out the view of the stars.
You are an old soul. Your ladders are poorly aged.
And all you can do is imagine what down looks like when you see a ladder going by.
You keep calling yourself Hope.
I am not hopeful for you.
The word denizen is not hopeful. And that's what you're full of.
Yes, you were built on the side of a mountain. Every year, you start to fall off the mountain.
Then, just in time, you catch hold of a ladder.
Maybe that's the extent of what you call hope.

# The drapery in most Renaissance paintings needs attendants to keep it in order

· · · · · · · · · · · · · · · · · · ·

Air in a cathedral has a feeling like living creatures when they are breathing.
Everything breathing being held in one place.
Like silence inside a viola before it is played.
Or whatever place it is in short stories that we refer to as the present tense.
A silence shared among people, when they're attached to their feelings and it involves
    everywhere they are looking.

In one church in Venice, you can see the Virgin Mary painted like it was a cardboard.
She's painted to look like a young girl.
Sit still, little girl. God is watching you.
For there is air being held still by attendants in waiting. Drapery, too. They brought it in
    for the background.
I learned about breathing at a church in Venice. It was very silent in there.
Attendants had arrived and they held my lungs still.
So the air could be circulating. How many airs are circulating in a man's lungs?

Holy! Holy! Holy! God of power. It might be God is breathing in there so I can feel even
    more.
Moving my insides the way breathing is supposed to happen.
Holding me together. Holding my insides in, too.
Like an inside of Mary with the inside of God that was inside Mary long enough
to see Mary the feeling creature feel her God an inside of God breathing,
like there's a certain rhythm when He's breathing
which is how people are breathing when they're trying to make babies.
God and Mary were making a baby.
"Keep the baby, Mary." That's what God said. "This one's on me."

One reason people are breathing in a cathedral is to make it where they believe the way
  Mary believed.
I can hear that while the air is being held in one place.
Attendants are watching. They have been all along.
And they have their own breathing.
The whole cathedral feels breathing. The definition of together began in a cathedral.
Aging, too. That's what a cathedral is. Aging.
With a portrait of Mary inside that is difficult to determine whether it's aging very well.

# The history I'm living in right now!

. . . . . . . . . . . . . . . . . . . . . . .

I was at a gallery in Europe where part of the exhibit required the corners of a room be
    removed.
The room was located in the middle of history.
Like there was one history that could happen to you in this room.
A constant history, like when a sculptor is cupping more clay onto your body,
so the underneath part of you starts to feel like an artifact.
But all you can think is what would it possibly mean if a part of your body was dug up out
    of your body?
And someone was saying, "Look. This was a part of your body!"

The gallery was showing the model of a city submerged and then periodically risen from
    the depths
so the water could cascade down the sides of buildings
and completely drench the models of fully grown trees.
Somewhere in that city is a model of you. With two pieces of coal for your eyes.
We're just about to meet. But, then, we're always about to meet, which is very exciting
    for the sculpture.
And especially us!

The fact is I didn't want to leave this room.
Because I like looking at a sculpture of me where I'm looking so casual.
Oh, look! A city has just been raised from the bottom of a body of water.
It is a constant history. With hands involved cupping my various body parts.
Careful hands around the careful body parts, please.

Hands willing to write about this room for me.
I'm in a pleasurable moment right now. Please, don't interrupt.
History is now. And then now. It's still happening now. And it appears it's all about me.
Do you hear the engines beneath the model of the city giving out?

Don't let them.

You and I are almost about to meet at the corner.

How much our history will change then! Were we almost about to change just a
     moment ago?

How much I'm dreading anything that will change what I'm doing right now.

All these hands touching in all the right places!

# What we did about a world that kept getting very loud

· · · · · · · · · · · · · · · · · · · · · · · · · · · · · · · · · · · · ·

We quit listening. All the listening was done. Listening, as an activity, had only occurred in
  the past tense.
We had mouths now. Vehicular mouths.
An ocean was being built from new mouths. Human mouths carved off their cadavers' faces.
Children's mouths. An orangutan's mouth puckering up at the camera.
That's how orangutans say I love you.
There was a God of Mouths who appeared as we were starting construction.
He offered us a sack of mouths, but none of them were His own.

What an ocean! Mouths on mouths.
Mouths engorged by the various rainstorms that wander over the ocean.
Though the rain made clear it wanted nothing to do with mouths.
But everyone knows rain is a part of nature. And nature, by its very nature, is related to
  thirst.
Some mouths preferred not to speak.
One well-placed smirk could be known to launch a thousand ships.
We blew up a giant balloon, and we held it in one place.
It felt like an ocean trying to keep it there.
But it was only a balloon hovering over a stadium.
Not the blimp kind. But a new invention designed to look much warmer after we wrapped
  it in cashmere.
We painted a mouth on the side of it. It looked like it was breathing.

No one had planned for how long it would take mouths to accumulate into an ocean.
When would there ever be enough mouths?
We were hoping there would be time for our children's children to have the pleasure of
  vacationing at a well-known beach.
Children are very loud at the beach.
They play with anything. It doesn't matter what it looks like.

It could be a mouth that reminds them of their grandmother.

Gorged with rainwater.

And swollen with bruises, because the other mouths had been kissing it over miles and miles of gentle ocean-rolling action.

I saw my grandmother's mouth the day after she died, and it was a very quiet mouth, a delicate mouth.

I wouldn't want to be looking at it while I was at the beach on vacation.

How much of my life did I live by virtue of my grandmother's mouth saying so much?

Now she is dead.

There should be nothing at all interesting about the familiarity of a mouth.

# A marriage procedure that involves quite a bit of my wife

(1) If my wife were holding a pumice stone in her hand, and (2) we had decided to stay in
   for the night,
(3) to reimagine a chandelier using pumice stones, or something more dense, like sandstone,
then (4) you might understand how our marriage works.

It constructs all the walls of the apartment.
It moves the north wall to the east corner. It circulates the air in our bedroom.
The carbon air.
The air that will have to be used a few times before it escapes into the outside part of our
   apartment.

Is it OK if I have hidden things in the air? Like clandestine music. Sometimes my wife.
How about the chair that I used to have at my desk before I bought a fancy one that has
   armrests?

What are all the inventories that get kept in the air?
My wife and I talk to each other a lot.
And we have long stretches where the words that the air has been holding are hidden,
or just below the surface, or in time with one another, or joking.
Plenty of times the words are just joking while they hang around the apartment.

When we are happy we take off our shirts.
We lie down in different rooms. And we talk from that far away.
So our voices can carry.

Devotion and exultation and compartmentalization and infatuation and insinuation are all
   products of these conversations.
Part of the tone of our voices. We are rough stones.
And the part that no one seems to understand is how easily we can stand beneath a
   chandelier
holding delicate wineglasses without the glass ever breaking.

## Maybe this city needs more men who are not imitations of the man they hate me for not being

• • • • • • • • • • • • • • • • • • • • • • • •

What does it mean when everyone you know has been fashioned using performance
    reviews
rather than a professional construction crew?
Or what do you do when you finally feel like you're responsible for the city's electrical grid,
and all you can hire is the wrong end of a ballpoint pen?
I'm pulling together a work zone, people.
First on the list, piece together a city,
not a conservatory, not a hothouse, not a well-manicured university.

I'm not sure what to say is sufficient for the project at hand.
I was given two hands and a full heart.
I was allotted an ocean, but only the parts zoned residential.
When I was 27, a book with some embarrassing fantasies was published as print-on-
    demand.
But who pays attention to a guy who's 27?

The peace of this world is in balsa wood.
Models of bridges. Flotation devices.
Imagine how you would feel if you could float down a river
and pretend your head was detached by all the people who hate you,
and the whole time you were singing,
and the animals mourned you, though mainly they just saw you as a delicious treat.
Such is the fate, apparently, of most American poets.
That is the sound of balsa wood. It was the destiny of this country when it was
    27 years old.

There will be a day when we will have to repopulate this city.
And I should not be the one who is left here to do it.

For I will bring in a small people.
Like they were the little plastic grasses you buy at Easter.
Who are thin. Negligible. They will feel like conditional statements.
For they will never be satisfied.

"I am not of you," I will declare.
I suppose that is what I've been declaring all along.

# Really, there is no end to ambition

· · · · · · · · · · · · · · · · · · · · · · · ·

I was a son. My house was a son. The city I walked in, the schoolbooks, the unexpected
  enlistment in the United States Navy, my career as a technical writer, my life in the
  public eye.
They were all sons fathered by other men. And then they were mine.
At least, for a moment.
But I was not to inherit a son.

In the tradition of my family, that starts with a single line drawn the length of a hallway,
there is one direction. And you never find out where it ends.

I inherited a staircase.
I carry it around. I wait at the bus stop on the top of my staircase. I go to the library
  where only staircases are allowed.
I plan special evenings with my wife where I put the staircase right between us,
so we can hardly see one another. "I'm looking straight at a staircase. Where are you?"

·

When I was a boy, my father gave up three of his fingers so he could inherit a son.
He told the whole world he would make him a failure.
For there is nothing more cruel than success.

Success is like a sky that was never allowed any staircases. Where do you go, then?
How long do you stay?
And when you breathe in how do you know the sky going into you is the sky
that was the meant for you sky, or at least the meant for that one part of you that could
    fit sky,
like if it was the sky in your lungs. Most people call that sky wish or determination,
or maybe they call it that one time in your life something good happened and you knew it
    was going to be the start of something real.
The future, the sky in your chest was the future.

I'd breathed it in.
Then I inherited a staircase. I named it Ambition.
And now I'm just a man who won't inherit a son.
Think of a home that was built a long time ago in a college town.
They converted it into apartments a few years ago. And they built a staircase on the outside.
What would the end be like for that home? How often does it feel embarrassed just to be
    standing?

•

How is it you're supposed to raise a staircase in this day and age?
When my staircase was young, I built it a nursery. I put a planet inside there.
A planet that was just forming.
Which can be dangerous.
My wife told me I'd need to make the walls thicker.
Thicker like thick concrete at the base of a tall building.

A staircase can't breathe. It doesn't need to breathe. We kept being afraid when it didn't
    breathe. We thought at least our staircase would breathe.

We had built a nursery where nothing could breathe.
That's how you make a staircase feel right at home.
You'll grow up a straight line, staircase. You'll always be a line in this family.

## They would excavate stones and then rearrange the stones in a city like they appeared in the earth

. . . . . . . . . . . . . . . . . . . . . .

The first time a medieval castle was built it was done using people.
Or the backs of people.
Who were in love with each other enough.
So they made a city. Using their arms and hands.
To sculpt the torsos and necks of considerate gods. To name the gods stones.
And stand the gods on the outside of the city.
Where they could look inside at the people.

Inside, the people always had other people laboring.
Beneath their skin metal splinters were reacting to the first part of the body.
So the ridges beneath the skin rose to appear on top of the skin.

A coat of arms should make you feel that new body inside your body there are many
    bodies.
We are grateful for how well bodies build into bodies.
Strong laborers are the people who must love one another for 1,000 years.
Like they love other people inside their city.
So long as they're named after their city.

# My fear is that someone would invent a tool to untether me

. . . . . . . . . . . . . . . . . . . . . . . . . . . . . . . . . . . . . .

I jumped against the sky expecting I would find another sky. A subtlety to sky.

I wanted to get to know the sky better. I wanted to breathe in the air. The sky as a blank
space.

Or maybe the opening to a decent conversation.

If you're using a camera you can pose against the sky and people will think that you're
flying.

Which is very dishonest.

Particularly to the sky.

Have you known a sky? I am trying to make its acquaintance.

The sky I am thinking of is a set piece for honesty.

Look into the night sky. All it is is confused.

The sky is revealing to the people what a sky can really look like.

Not day. Not the sky that's being suspended over the whole state of Texas.

Just estranged populations.

So many populations running away from the earth.

I don't know what to do about a sky when it's like this.

I am more a middle of the day. My favorite meal is lunch.

My favorite tree is whatever it is that is happening in the spring, mainly after a strong
rain.

Maybe sometimes when the leaves change.

So long as the place I'm living in is conducive to trees.

Their weights and measurements. Their various relationships with a sky.

Is there a place where birds come from? I think it's the sky.

A tree absorbs sky. It takes it into its lungs.

How sky is sky? say the trees. And that seems to mean something.

I built a house, and I made sure there was one window.

I nailed a tether to the side of that window. On the outside, I put sky.

I was jumping to the outside so many times I forgot what falling is in a sky.

I am coming for you, Sky!

Do not misinform me or take me into account. I was attached to this house for a reason.

Sometimes I jump, and I am air.

Then I am sky.

I think, "And, now, everything else!" Where everything else is the order of sky.

Air molecules. Air molecules existing. All they can do is keep existing.

# An ellipsis could be what language is like when it's styrofoam

. . . . . . . . . . . . . . . . . . . . . . . . . . . . . . . . . . . . . .

A leg made of styrofoam is barely a leg.

Which is what it feels like when you have your knee taken away from you.

Your leg is only kind of attached.

And your stomach starts to fill with styrofoam.

And your breath actually gets populated by styrofoams.

Fortunately, they gave me another leg. But it was still only styrofoam.


Fortunately, because up to this point my leg had required so much scaffolding that I was
    unable to speak clearly.

The scaffolding was an elaborate celebration.

Like Berlin in the 1990s, when it was being rebuilt.

And all of the streets were scaffolding.

Along with the fastest automobiles.

Along with the news stations, and all the news crews.

Scaffolded together so that you could understand how complicated the full story was even
    after just 30 minutes of air time.


How do you remind yourself that life is constructing without any thought about the
    materials you're being given?

I live in mountains, among mountains, between mountains. And my only relationship is to
    a tree.

I don't care that there are many trees here.

I need help. Like, just with the walking part.

Before my hands are styrofoam. Or my arms. And I'm falling down.

With that tree I know laughing at me.

Because a tree doesn't fall. At least that's what the tree thinks.

.

In first grade, I made a model of the solar system using styrofoam balls. They were all painted to look like different planets. And the sun, too. And I didn't win anything for it. But I knew what the solar system knew. Outer space is special and quiet and I had discovered a quiet victory when I made it all look like styrofoam.

I was running out of the school with it. I was trying to run faster than the wind that kept picking it up from my hands. Why couldn't I run faster than the wind? Because I was 6 years old. And the wind was malicious. It took the solar system away from me. You live on earth, the wind said. That is the picture of my education. The picture of me running, but never as fast as the wind.

. . .

## "I want to give you a spring." I said to my wife.
## And my wife only listened.

· · · · · · · · · · · · · · · ·

So I rented a truck, and I filled it with containers.

I labeled them "listening."

Then I drove to the park to collect 16 oz. of air.

Then another 16 oz. And another. Air only with air usually, because that's how it is with air.

But sometimes air circulating beside new leaves.

Air inside a bird's mouth. Air beside the white chickens.

There were soil samples, too. 16 oz. deep.

16 oz. of trees. Many different trees. And 16 oz. of ducks.

"One day spring will end." Of course it will, said the containers.

But why should I care?

I have so many ounces of spring. I am listening to the spring.

And the title of this installation isn't "Reason." The title is "100%."

The time where air actually starts feeling like it might be lighter than air. We can call it
    enthusiasm.

Containers of air floating a few feet off the ground.

And that made room for containers of trees.

And benches. Only 16 oz. of benches?

No. I had many containers of each section of park.

A whole category of containers. Sometimes for each kind of air. Not so many for redbuds.

They were later than usual that year.

Parked cars. And children. And laughter. All in containers.

Labeled and numbered.

Can you imagine a painting of a park, and people enjoying the spring in a park?

You might call that painting "An Animal Majesty."

Or 16 oz. of always beginning. Added, multiplied, and arranged.
What exactly is it that factorials measure? Somewhere around 100%. Maybe more.


My wife arrived, and she took a container of air and put it under containers of geese.
The geese took flight.
The two of us were standing on either side of the containers labeled "a river runs
    through it."
They call this a pastoral setting. They call this a park in this city.
How much of our living was going to be starting right there. During spring.
It would be exactly like it was spring.

# This is how ambition looks when it's blooming

· · · · · · · · · · · · · · · · · · · · · · · · · · · · · ·

We were a forest. We were a collection of young trees that had been grown inside a
    museum.
To look like a forest, they had opened our skin with hooks.
And dug into our skin with hooks.
We appeared aged. And professional. Our arms full of leaves, but the leaves were brittle.
We barely wanted to look at each other while this was happening.
We begged them. Don't let anyone know we are here.

That's almost how a forest works.
But a forest is outside. Most of it's been drawn on with crayons and rubber cement. People
    are leaving pictures of someone they know.
Or something valuable you'd want to remember in a forest.
Like running. Like winds pulling and dying and getting tangled.
And winds eventually returning.

We had been young trees. Very young. They had left the hooks there for weeks.
We can take it. We said.
There was this sculpture by Michelangelo where he trapped slaves inside a piece of marble.
It could have been titled "Institution." But it was only slaves.
We were supposed to be better than that. Breathing. Like there was wind in our lungs.
    Breathing.

I wish I could convince someone how valuable a life experience can be.
They had bought safety pins to keep the leaves attached to our shoulders.
They were very quiet around us.
The us that was inside us was magnificent structures. And they weren't going to grow any
    larger.
We would be decorated with miniature fauna they had brought in to fool people.
A terracotta deer with amethyst for an eye. A fox. But I think the fox might have been real.

# I was born a bass drum. Not a catapult.

· · · · · · · · · · · · · · · · · · · · · · · ·

The people I know could never afford to employ the roster of spies that I have.
I have spies for my dinnerware. Spies that inspect the olives I like eating in the afternoon.
Spies for the cat litter, both content and quality of discharge.
I have spies for eloquence. If only the spies by themselves were eloquent.
They are very numerous, however.
I have spies living in the little hut I built to keep them in my living room.
My wife doesn't mind.
They are mostly millimeter spies. And pantry spies. And get Kent invited to the party spies.
I can sometimes be ineffectual.

Which wouldn't matter if I had only been born a bass drum. I wasn't.
I'm sorry if you were led to believe otherwise.
And now I have a need for spies who can keep white lies like this safe.

·

There is a catapult on my front lawn. I put it there so I would have something to model
    my life after.
I've not yet taught it eloquence. Which is unfortunate.
However, it didn't come with any ammunition.
It's barely zoned for this residence.
I had to tell the city that it operates like a flock of birds
that appear from a distance to be moving in one slow, continuous motion,
but when you look more closely, you can see each bird is panicked,
because it might not have the strength to keep up with the other birds around it.
My catapult has a lot to live up to.

I'm hoping we will both grow up to be what people call an alienated civilization.
Where everyone is watching us, but they won't tell me what they see.
I am empty. I know. On good days, I'm silent. Some might say I'm inert.

But I have potential. Just look at this whole lifestyle of potential.
I have spies. I have birds. I have millimeters in every part of my life.
My life is a bass drum. At least that's what I'm telling people.
Is it possible to be a successful over-dependent?
A catapult that is so fenced in by what it depends on
the city can safely pretend it just doesn't exist?

# The definition of OK when you're only kind of OK

· · · · · · · · · · · · · · · · · · · · · · · · · · · · ·

It means the things that fit into a box are not shaped like a box.
I tried making "fix" the size of a box.
I held it over the lid, like I was measuring it out.
I'm taking this "fix" with me to my next apartment, where I plan to live by myself.
This "fix" should fit around my cat's abdomen.
It was shaved two weeks ago to make room for another abdomen.
When the vet asked me what was inside the box, I pointed to the calendar.
But that didn't fix anything.

All the things that fit into a box are not shaped like a box.
A newish marriage is still so new it could pretty much fit in a box.
But you don't want it to look like a box.
My investment portfolio.
My new tie, even though it is orange or peach depending on who you're asking.
I'm trying to tell the story of giving unconditionally. But with certain conditions.

You're not supposed to keep all your things in a box if they're important to you.
Like you were planning to move away.
I'm tired of pretending to be flexible. Or versatile.
I have been living a life shaped like boxes. My voice taped shut inside a box.
My morning. My trip to the grocery store.
There are many boxes stacking up. Is there anything that could fix this?

# To mountainize is a verb

. . . . . . . . . . . . . .

The mountains have been moving. They have been evolving, but they're not telling anyone.
That's the nature of the earth.
A whole technology all the time moving.
They are a herd of mountains. They are herds of American bison.

Imagine a beast. Imagine how a beast feels on the inside.
What is it holding on to?
Achilles was a man who could pretend he was a beast when it mattered.
For him, it usually mattered.
What is the beast living inside a mountain?

We are complicated creatures,
looking for new ways of looking, and having, and keeping, and memorizing, and practicing,
and please remembering just one more thing
that I don't appreciate remembering as much as I probably should.

My mother was a mountain among mountains. And then she was laid low.
That was the time of Apocalypse.
My father was always laboring for the mountain he told me was on the inside of a
    mountain.
And now he is tired. But not the luxurious tired.

My genetic history is part concord part chasm.
I tell the people in this mountainous state I was descended from beasts,
because no single beast is satisfied by the look of other beasts, even if corralled into good
    working order,
and told what technology would efficiently coordinate their efforts.

These are the conditions for how I was born.
I was dancing. What is rage but dancing?
What is all my fury to the insides of these mountains that aren't letting me go?

# The title of this drawing would be "the prime of your life"

. . . . . . . . . . . . . . . . . . . . . . . . . . . . . . . . .

It is difficult to be living with the prime of your life. It's the first part of your life you
   watch die.
There are people in my life I should explain this to.
I am dying. What a luxury.
Every day, I am still dying.
But I have too many family obligations to really be serious.
Though I must be. I will be. I am meaning to be.

There have been other people I know who took dying seriously.
Dying takes a lot of energy to get started.
Or so goes the poetry written by John Keats.

I remember in the 70s watching a gorilla throw up in its cage.
I was laughing when it started eating it off the floor.
Maybe the gorilla was being a serious creature signaling its own needs.
"That could be you," I said to my father.
But why would either one of us have a conversation about dying if we were both enjoying
   the prime of our lives?

I am often thinking about that awkward pause when a friend makes an important
   announcement.
It is difficult to be the center of attention at times like this.
It's like living in a cage.
I would rather it be I'm living in a community of cages.
Where all of us are dying at our own pace.
I just wanted everyone to know. I'm in the beginning of the beginning of my middle life.
This is dying.
And my middle life is dying even while it begins.

# Actually, this poem belongs to my wife

· · · · · · · · · · · · · · · · · · · · · · · · ·

There were the arms that were grown inside a woman
without asking whether arms are what she was hoping her womanhood would be filled by.
What were the arms trying to find in this woman?

Arms are like disciples. They are disciples.
Jesus lined his twelve disciples along the wall and He held a piece of ham at their face, each
    face,
and He said, "This is my body!"
No one believed Him. And so He went looking for a more subtle analogy.

But arms find it hard to know what they should believe.
Moving inside a woman's shirt like they were looking for something.
To swim requires a powerful set of arms.
Is it any coincidence that women are typically better swimmers than men?
Imagine if arms had been created with eyes.

A man who has a box of tools in his trunk will throw every single tool from one side of the
    car to the other in order to find the 9/16" wrench.
Who is the disciple in this case?
It is a known fact that Jesus threw a piece of ham right at Judas' face.
And so Judas betrayed Him.

What was life like for arms when they were younger?
When she was young, did the woman hold them at night with her human arms?
Did she have lullabies to sing about climbing smaller trees that were growing somewhere
    else in the city?
Were there swings close by? How do you swing when you have more than two arms?

# What we do when we want to elect a Frank Lloyd Wright

First, build a terrace that is built from the other terraces in your neighborhood,
because you should start out looking very high.
Like you were looking for the beginnings of the Midwest or Baltimore.
Or the beginnings of multiplication or discipline.
What do you begin with at a beginning?
Probably not questions.
The men I hired are making fun of me because they are much higher than I am right now.
And I'm leading by example.
Frank Lloyd Wright built Fallingwater so that there was as much square footage of terrace
    as there was indoor space.
And he didn't even care about presidents.

Not like I do. I'm a ewe in sheep's clothing. I'm a persuasive argument.
I'm a parachute that's been packed away for portability.
Which is to say I'm the most sinewy motherfucker you're going to meet who's building a
    terrace
that piles on top of other terraces so that there's no question where the top of the whole
    United States is.
And it takes a steady eye to see high enough where it's all supposed to come together.

·

I could put the Midwest in Baltimore.
Though I'd leave my hometown in the middle of this country.
And I'd leave Atlanta in Georgia. Because Atlanta doesn't like to be messed with.

But in the end I'm only building a terrace. It will look like a bridge.
But more like bridges crossing over other bridges.
I see it like a treehouse that keeps getting multiplied by the sky.
That doesn't allow children to live inside, though, because of the shoddy construction.
That looks like raised highways piled one on top of the other so that whatever decorative
    elements had been molded in the concrete probably got pushed down by the weight.
And everything could collapse at any moment.

# How to rule out probability

. . . . . . . . . . . . . . . . .

To adequately birth a square word, I had to acquire a square tongue.
That wouldn't fit in my mouth.
I removed my mouth. I removed my nostrils to make some more room.
I hired an artist who could draw my nose to the side of my face,
like when you aren't sure which is the best way to look in a mirror.

And as I struggled to learn, all squares became squarer.
Square prison cells.
Square chair inside built from raised concrete
that they painted gray so you know it's different from the floor.

Do I have to paint myself white?
Do I have to make part of my body a floor?

There are always going to be sacrifices when you're becoming a soul.
Oh, miserable souls.
But it wasn't dark in this prison. It was the suburbs.
Most varieties of fluorescent light were invented in the suburbs.
And the toy window, too, that lets you see the insides of things.

I am not sure how much more I can make a square with my body.
Or why squares require so much square to work right.
Are there other squares available?
Have all the best squares been rented out already?
How many different squares has a square evolved to before it was the square of today?
How much longer will I be waiting?

# The sense that balsa wood isn't really the best decision

There was the balsa wood ankles that we had substituted for our ankles.

We thought it would tickle. Or be educational.

A world of colorful street signs.

Colorful stores with many of the people inside colored to feel balsa wood in their faces and their fingers handing currency over to the cashier.

The colors that we have to believe in are inside the balsa wood.

The ceiling shaped like a teardrop and pushing some people into the floor.

That makes it a little uncomfortable.

Buildings aren't supposed to have teardrops inside them.

But then nothing is stable. Even walking isn't stable.

The staircases had turned against people trying to climb up.

Where are you going? And now you're probably not going to remember where you had come from.

I thought tying my shoes would sort things out.

The ceilings would raise up and give the rooms a little air when they leapt off the walls.

I am sorry. I can't run any faster.

I can't build a wall and a job to attach to the wall and flurries of cotton candy disintegrating when you throw it into the rain.

I am sorry. My ankles are giving out. The colors are giving out. There will only be rain.

A ceiling that's raining and pressing my arms onto the sand.

Like under the sand. Where the sand gives in to my body.

And then it's both sand and rain once I'm below ground. They are pushing me harder and harder.

These are the colors I prefer.

# When your middle age is in the middle beginning

· · · · · · · · · · · · · · · · · · · · · · · · · · · ·

And what do you make an atmosphere out of?
Lead. Lead curtains. Lead coughing fits that could give you an excuse to stay in bed.
Lead croissants. I'm having a hard time with 40.

And an even harder time with 41. The sea is lead when you look at it during a storm.
Or when you're drowning.
Is it really so unlikely that there would be so much lead?

Let me introduce you to 40: The mountains that exist opposite my house. My wife who is
    so young. The flowers they sell at the grocery store. Sometimes they are chrysanthemums.
And they are always the same color.
Let us all sing together! Unanimous!

All the atmospheres. And the household gods.
And all the 40-year-olds who exist despite the atmosphere that is only incidentally alive
    in the atmosphere.
Around us and between us. Beneath us, too, when we're driving.

There is a storm made of atmospheres, and it's threatening the mourning doves.
And the single conifer they're living in, which isn't enough shelter.
Lead is a poison. It is a deadliness.
What do you do when you're covered in lead?
You don't breathe. Not for one second.

# A dramatic reenactment to explain why the internet was started

I was hired by government workers to make drawings of the internet.
They said, "Make it a silk knot."
I drew a portrait instead. It looked like George Washington.
A knot is so quiet and subtle and perspicuous.
I proposed, Let the internet be a crew of electricians shouting at one another.
They could be holding electrical cables.
And they would be telling each other everything that is or is not happening "inside the
     network."

My problem is I don't know if any of the electricians left really like me.
I was never a good electrician.
I was the one who left a job site with something important, like a 9/16" wrench.
Like I would have been a better electrician if I was walking through the neighborhood with
     a shopping cart full of extension cords.
"Fellow travelers, I am a traveler."
"Fellow governments, I am a government grant."

The dramatic reenactment they used on the 11 o'clock news.
Any actual footage is so uneventful, it probably doesn't exist.
And yet I am right here. In the middle of everything.

•

Before the internet there was a tree. And there were only a few branches on the tree.
No one could see whether the tree was happy.
But that's because no one cares about a tree.
People are waiting around for something they can care about.
I have extension cords, I said.
I have Christmas lights on my truck. I will drive up and down your block if you plug me in.
And we can yell, "Internet!" at the top of our lungs.

Would you believe the government had already thought about the internet in the 1970s?
    Or even 1980 before Ronald Reagan became president?
The people then had a different understanding of why.
Why the government would buy someone a truck.
Why artistic value and fast food and unleaded gasoline would have to be a part of the
    production.
Governments in the 70s were sensitive to the people's needs.
The governments loved the people.
They combed the people's hair and said soothing things to them while they fell asleep at
    the TV.

Why do things always change?
Governments are always growing such exorbitant proofs,
where trees are planted on top of other trees and the capitol building gets remade from
    street lamps
twisted into the joined profile of Thomas Jefferson and Sally Hemings in a passionate kiss.
Isn't this the actual country we keep trying to fit inside the one that we're living in?
Thomas Jefferson devoted himself to feeling a special kind of free.
It was so special he chose to keep every bit of it for himself.

# JUNIPER
JUNIPER PRIZE FOR POETRY

This volume is the forty-fourth recipient of the
Juniper Prize for Poetry, established in 1975 by the
University of Massachusetts Press in collaboration with
the UMass Amherst MFA program for Poets and Writers.
The prize is named in honor of the poet Robert Francis
(1901–1987), who for many years lived in Fort Juniper,
a tiny home of his own construction, in Amherst.